SHADOW WORK JOURNAL

An Intuitive Guide to Help you Find Inner Peace and Happiness Through Self-Discovery

Written by

MICHELLE CHIRA

To anyone out there who is struggling to accept themselves,

I want you to know that you are not alone. This workbook is for you. It will guide you through the process of self-acceptance and growth.

You are brave for embarking on this journey, and I believe in you.

Table of Contents

Introduction

It's constantly just behind us, just out of sight. We cast a shadow in any direct light.

The shadow is a psychological word for everything in ourselves that we cannot see. Most of us will go to considerable measures to shield our self-image from anything unattractive or strange. As a result, observing another's shadow is simpler than noticing one's own.

When writing a spiritual teacher biography, I realized how vital understanding my shadow was. Seeing this teacher's shadow helped me comprehend how someone might be gifted in one area of life while being unconscious of terrible conduct in another.

Every person is vulnerable to this.

Working with my shadow is a wonderful yet challenging experience. Exploring your shadow may lead to increased honesty, creativity, vitality, and awareness.

Shadow work is the practice of facing your shadow self and releasing what's holding you back. This all-in-one shadow work journal contains exercises and guided journal prompts to help you engage with the shadows and face the future with peace and confidence.

We put a lot of effort into trying to create the best journal on the market that can help you discover a part of yourself that usually remains hidden.

The journal is divided into five main sections:

1) Understanding what is Shadow Work
2) Your Journey Into Shadow Work
3) The Workbook, Shadow Exercises
4) Letters to Self
5) Shadow Prompts

Each section will progressively guide you through your journey of self-discovery. The first two parts will set the guidelines for your work while the last three contain a variety of exercises and journal prompts designed to help you get in touch with your shadow self, understand what's holding you back, and release your shadows.

We hope that this shadow work journal will help you on your journey of self-discovery and personal growth.

Part 1 Introduction to Shadow Work

"The shadow is needed now more than ever. We heal the world when we heal ourselves, and hope shines brightest when it illuminates the dark."

- Sasha Graham

What is the Shadow?

Shadow work is the psychological process of bringing unconscious parts of the self into conscious awareness. It is a form of inner work that can be beneficial for anyone, but it is especially helpful for people who have experienced trauma or who are struggling with mental health issues. Shadow work can be uncomfortable, but it is worth trying because it can lead to profound insights and healing. Through shadow work, we can learn to embrace all aspects of ourselves, even the parts that we may find ugly or painful. In doing so, we can become more whole and complete human beings.

Your shadow self is the part of you that lives in your subconscious and houses your darkest thoughts, such as limiting beliefs and traumatic memories. This shadow work journal contains advice and guided journal prompts to help you engage with the shadows and face the future with peace and confidence.

Because your shadow self contains your deepest fears and insecurities, it can profoundly impact your life. If you don't deal with your shadow self, it can lead to problems like anxiety, depression, and substance abuse. Shadow work can help you confront your fears and overcome them.

How the Shadow is Born

Shadow Work is a psychological concept first conceived by Swiss psychiatrist Carl Jung. It refers to the parts of ourselves that we are not conscious of or that we tend to repress. This can include anything from our dark impulses and desires to our more positive qualities that we are afraid to embrace. The shadow can be seen as the "bad" side of our personality but consequentially also the side that contains greater potential for growth and transformation. By becoming aware of our shadow, we can learn to accept all aspects of ourselves, both light and dark. This can lead to a greater sense of self-awareness and personal power. Shadow Work is an ongoing process that requires courage and vulnerability, but the rewards can be bountiful.

While Jung may have been the first to invent the term "shadow self," the notion of inner self-awareness has existed for as long as humans have. Self-evaluation for personal and spiritual development is mentioned in ancient spiritual literature, many of which are being utilized today as instructions for living a wholesome and well-rounded life.

As evidenced by the New Thought and New Age spiritual movements, the ability of one to introspect and develop their own consciousness if they so choose to put in the work has formed the foundation of many modern-day spiritual doctrines.

The field of psychology has grown increasingly fascinated by the idea of the unconscious mind and the role it may play in human behavior. Austrian neurologist Sigmund Freud was one of the first to propose the existence of an unconscious mind, and his theories continue to be influential today. The unconscious mind is thought to be a storehouse of repressed memories, desires, and impulses outside of our conscious awareness. However, these hidden forces can still exert a powerful influence on our behavior. Psychologist operating under the umbrella of psychoanalytic theory believe that understanding the unconscious mind can help us to better understand ourselves and make more informed decisions in our day-to-day lives. As such, the study of the unconscious mind remains a key area of research within psychology.

Why You Should Get to Know Your Shadow

Some individuals find it difficult to honor the darkness. After all, the night is often linked with peril, and our forefathers had every cause to be concerned about ambush in their sleep. However, shamans from several cultures see the night as the ideal time to communicate with our spirit guides for healing and development. The darkness serves as a blank canvas for us to cast our anxieties, doubts, and concerns. We may only begin to shed our worries and move ahead into the light by deliberately confronting them in the darkness.

Honoring the darkness in this way may be a vital step on the journey to self-discovery and personal improvement.

While the ego mind, that part of the human personality that is perceived as the "self" or "I" and has contact with the outside world via perception, likes to perceive things in terms of black and white, the truth is that both darkness and light are essential aspects of existence and the human experience. Without darkness, we would not be able to appreciate the beauty of light. And without light, we would not be able to see the shadows that provide depth and dimension to our lives. As we begin to let go of our judgmental views of these energies, we open ourselves up to a more expansive understanding of reality. We no longer see darkness as something to be feared, but rather as an integral part of the whole. In doing so, we become more accepting of ourselves and of the world around us.

The shadow was first defined as something that was hidden from the light or shaded. In the mid-14th century, the word came to represent something perceived as evil, such as a ghost or dark entity. Because the word is often associated with doom and gloom, it can bring up uncomfortable feelings due to subconscious associations. When addressing the shadow, we must address duality. There is always a balance between the light and the dark. Everyone has tucked-away secrets, private thoughts they dare not speak of, and unrevealed desires. Collectively, there has always been a yearning to explore this hidden realm of the psyche, which is why the shadow archetype has always been such a prominent character in much of our literature, theater, and films, think Dr. Jekyll and Mr. Hyde.". By understanding and embracing our shadow side, we can achieve a more balanced and healthy state of being.

What Happens When You Repress Your Shadow?

So, what happens to all the bits of ourselves that we hide?

We perceive in others the traits we ignore in ourselves. This is known as projection in psychology. We transfer onto others whatever we hide inside ourselves.

If you feel annoyed when someone is disrespectful to you, chances are you haven't owned your own rudeness. This individual may be unpleasant; nevertheless, if rudeness and disrespect were not in your shadow, the rudeness of others would not affect you as much. This procedure does not take place intentionally. The majority of us are completely unaware of our projections. Our egos utilize this defense mechanism to safeguard our self-image and self-identity.

It works like this: beginning in early childhood, we begin psychically severing portions of ourselves. We distance ourselves from our finest qualities, such as courage, generosity, and compassion. And we disassociate with our worst traits, such as jealousy, pettiness, and wrath. We shut ourselves off from whatever we can't assimilate. We separate ourselves from everything that does not receive acceptance or approval from our surroundings, including our parents, teachers, relatives, and friends.

We aim to be "normal," ordinary in some ways. We seek the middle in order to fit in during childhood and adolescence — not our own middle, but the middle of our social groupings and society as a whole.

Unfortunately, our school systems promote this soul surgery.

These systems are extremely good at removing our innate genius, those attributes that set us apart from the "average." All of these characteristics are stored in what psychoanalysts refer to as the shadow. Or, as poet Robert Bly put it: an "invisible bag" we've been carrying about from childhood. Because we can't easily perceive these features in ourselves, our imaginations project them onto others. You are noticing your own selfishness when you become frustrated by his selfishness at work. However, your annoyance stems from your refusal to accept responsibility for your own selfishness.

You would not be annoyed if this were not the case. You would see your colleague's selfishness and quickly recognize your own selfishness. (Because we are all reflections of one another.) Instead, you have self-awareness-based knowledge. There would be no emotional trigger to annoy.

How Shadow Work Can Help You

Your connection with your shadow is one that lasts a lifetime, one that will call you for healing time and time again while providing you with a greater awareness of your entire self in the process. This is the essence of the human experience. The objective is to reach a place where you are always addressing the shadow with love, compassion, and, most importantly, gratitude for the things it may teach you.

Few people enjoy exploring their shadows. After all, the shadow contains all of our flaws, traumas, and blind spots It can be painful to face up to these aspects of ourselves. However, repression, denial, and other forms of avoidance are only temporary solutions. Eventually, our shadows will catch up with us.

Fortunately, there are many benefits to integrating our shadow selves. For one thing, it can lead to personal growth and development. By facing up to our negative qualities, we can learn to accept them and even make use of them. In addition, exploring the shadow can help us to build stronger relationships with others. When we understand our own shadows, we can be more understanding and compassionate towards the shadows of others. Finally, coming to terms with our shadows can give us a greater sense of self-acceptance and self-love.

Let's take a look at the advantages of incorporating your shadow:

Mental Wellbeing

When we are living unaware of our wounds, we tend to exist in a reactive state of fight-or-flight that often manifests as anxiety, depression, anger, and other forms of mental anguish. As we address and heal our unresolved wounds, we begin to break free from the chains of suffering. In doing Shadow Work, we open ourselves up to deeper levels of self-understanding and compassion. We also create space for joy, love, and vitality to flow more freely in our lives. As you become more comfortable with who you are, you will find it easier to let go of judgment and feelings of insecurity.

You will be able to approach your work with a more open and relaxed mindset. This will allow you to tap into your creativity and intuition, which will ultimately lead to better results. So, if you're feeling stuck in a rut, consider venturing into the shadows. It may just be the key to unlocking your full potential.

Social Connectivity

We all have things about ourselves that we would rather not face. Maybe we don't like the way we look, or maybe we're afraid of what other people will think if they find out about our past. Whatever the case may be, there are always parts of ourselves that we would rather keep hidden.

However, when we try to hide these aspects of ourselves, they often manifest in other ways. We might find ourselves being critical of others or lashing out in anger. Alternatively, we might find ourselves drawn to people who embody the very qualities that we are trying to hide. In either case, it is clear that these hidden parts of ourselves are having an impact on our lives. The first step in addressing this issue is to become more aware of what we are trying to hide.

Once we know what these hidden parts are, we can begin to work on accepting them. This can be a difficult process, but it is essential if we want to improve our relationships with others. When we commit to being more loving, accepting, and compassionate toward ourselves, we will naturally become more loving, accepting, and compassionate toward others as well. This automatically improves your interactions and strengthens all your relationships. So, the next time you find yourself being triggered by someone else's behavior, take a step back and ask yourself what you might be hiding from yourself. Chances are, you'll find that the answer lies within you.

Build and Develop Confidence

The personal development movement has conditioned us to look for external strategies for improving our confidence. Some of these strategies are effective, at least in the short term. For example, doing a Tony Robbins-style "power move" before giving a presentation to a group can help to subdue your fear of speaking, at least temporarily.

However, if you're not working on understanding and addressing the source of your anxiety, there will be no lasting change. Ultimately, authentic development occurs when you get to the root of this fear, accept it, and integrate it into your conscious personality. This happens in the course of getting to know and integrating your shadow. Working on understanding and accepting your shadow self is essential for developing lasting confidence.

Healing from Past Traumas

There is no better gift than healthy living. I have witnessed personally the metamorphosis that occurs when emotional wounds are healed. Unresolved trauma, no matter how old, festers, much like a physical sore that may get infected if not treated. The poisonous energy of unresolved wounds leads to subpar life. The willingness to repair previous wounds is the key to rising beyond the conditions of your existence. You must be willing to confront your fears, insecurities, and doubts in order to understand why they are there in the first place. Only then can you work on resolving them. Without this willingness, the cycle of unhealthy living will continue.

Achieving Your Goals

One of the biggest obstacles to achieving our goals is often ourselves. We might doubt our abilities or question whether we are worthy of achieving our desires. These negative thoughts can sabotage our efforts before we even get started. So how can we overcome these self-imposed limitations?

The answer lies in understanding and accepting our shadow selves. Our shadows contain all the aspects of ourselves that we have rejected. They represent our fears, doubts, and insecurities. By bringing these hidden parts of ourselves into the light, we can begin to understand and accept them. This process will ultimately help us to achieve our goals and realize our full potential.

Develop Self-Knowledge

It can be difficult to see ourselves and others objectively. We all have biases and perspectives that cloud our judgment. However, it is important to try to see things as they really are. Only then can we truly understand ourselves and others.

When we see things through a cleaner lens, we can approach our lives with greater clarity, compassion, and understanding. It is only by integrating the shadow selves that we can hope to achieve this goal. By accepting all aspects of ourselves—the good and the bad—we can start to see the world as it really is. And that is a beautiful thing.

Move Toward Psychological Integration (Wholeness)

Shadows exist as the rejected and suppressed parts of ourselves that we are unaware of. It's easy to understand why we try to keep these aspects hidden away. No one wants to think of themselves as being cruel, jealous, or manipulative. However, owning up to our shadows is an important part of self-awareness and growth. By integrating our shadows, we can begin to understand the motivations behind our actions. We can also start to see the impact that our repressed emotions have on our relationships and decision-making. Recognizing the power of our shadows can help us to create a more balanced and unified sense of self. In turn, this can lead to a greater sense of wholeness and peace in our lives.

The beauty of Shadow Work is that it's an ongoing journey of self-discovery. As you allow yourself to be vulnerable and explore the parts of yourself that you've been hiding away, you open up the opportunity for miraculous moments of growth and healing. It can be a difficult and challenging process, but it's also incredibly rewarding.

Each time you face your fears and dig deeper into your shadows, you emerge a little bit stronger and a little bit wiser. Over time, you'll start to see the world in a new light and discover aspects of yourself that you never knew existed. It's a lifelong journey, but one that is well worth taking.

Elevate Your Creativity

One of the major advantages of integrating your shadow is that it allows you to tap into more of your creative potential. Humanistic psychologists like Abraham Maslow and Carl Rogers discovered that creativity is a natural occurrence among mentally healthy (integrated) people. Similarly, Jung discovered that as people proceeded along their pathways of individuation, they began to participate in various types of creative self-expression.

This implies that integrating your shadow not only improves your mental health but also allows you to access previously untapped creative potential. As a result, if you want to tap into your entire creative potential, integrative work in your shadow is important. It will not only make you a more well-rounded and balanced person, but it will also help you to tap into previously unexplored elements of your personality and creativity.

Dissolve Internal Resistance to Change

Resistance is a term we use to describe internal tension. Internal tension means that our conscious mind is at odds with various parts within our unconscious. The purpose of shadow integration is to help bring these hidden parts to consciousness. And as we integrate these parts, these internal tensions begin to dissolve on their own. However, before this can happen, we first need to become aware of our shadows.

Our shadow contains all the aspects of ourselves that we are not consciously aware of. This includes both the positive and negative aspects of our personality. In order for us to grow and develop as individuals, it is essential that we learn to accept all parts of ourselves, both the light and the dark. Unfortunately, many of us have a tendency to repress or deny the existence of our shadow self.

As a result, we end up projecting these qualities onto others instead of dealing with them directly. This can lead to a lot of destructive behavior in our lives. By remaining unconscious to our shadow, we are effectively cut off from a large part of ourselves. And until we learn to face our shadow, we will continue to act out in ways that are harmful not only to ourselves but also to those around us.

Shadows Can be Scary!

But facing them is worth it! It's full of the things we don't want to see about ourselves. It's the part of us that is dark and ugly and full of shame. But if we can learn to confront our shadow, we can also learn to accept all parts of ourselves.

We can learn to love ourselves, our flaws, and all. And in doing so, we can also learn to love others more fully and completely. If you are feeling overwhelmed or lost, remember that you are not alone on this journey. There are others who have walked this path before you and there are resources available to help you. Reach out for help when you need it and take comfort in knowing that you are not alone.

There is no shame in asking to a good friend or a partner or a professional trainer for help to guide you through your Shadow Work journey. However, remember that your own inner guidance system is the best tool you have for doing this work. Pay attention to your emotional reactions and identify patterns to help you determine what needs to change. You may need to experiment with different approaches before you find what works best for you, but trust your instincts and let your heart be your guide.

It may also be helpful to talk to others who have gone through similar experiences and see how they coped. Ultimately, though, only you can know what will work best for you, so don't be afraid to listen to your heart and follow its lead.

Tips for Engaging Your Shadow

Here are seven things that will make incorporating your shadow simpler for you:

Cultivate Self-Awareness

Shadow Work can be difficult because it requires us to face parts of ourselves that we may not like or be proud of. However, the first step to Shadow Work is simply becoming aware of your own shadow. This starts with being **mindful and present** in the now, without judgment. Try not to get caught up in your thoughts or allow your inner critic to take over. Instead, observe your thoughts and feelings as they come and go.

Once you're able to do this, you can begin to reflect on your reactions to different situations. Why did you react that way? What triggers these reactions? As you start to answer these questions, you'll slowly begin to understand your shadow better. However, it's important to remain patient and nonjudgmental throughout this process. Remember that everyone has a shadow, and it's nothing to be ashamed of. Embrace it and use it as a tool for growth.

Cultivate Unwavering Self-Honesty

The practice of self-honesty is a necessary but difficult step in personal growth. Our early life experiences condition us to be deceptive to ourselves, making it difficult to break the habit. However, self-honesty and integrity are key to working with our shadow selves. Lip service is easy, but true self-honesty requires the willingness to see the unpleasant aspects of our behavior and personality that don't match up with our self-image.

This can be very uncomfortable and explains why the ego invests so much energy in repressing these parts of ourselves. For example, it can be challenging to accept our insecure selfishness or tyrannical tendencies—especially if we see ourselves as "good people."

The self-esteem movement of the 1970s was built on the idea that praising children would help them to develop a strong sense of self-worth. However, recent research has shown that this may not be the case. In fact, praising children indiscriminately can actually lead to a false sense of worth or inflation. This can ultimately mask insecurity or deflation, which can lead to difficult emotions and behaviors. However, taking an honest look at these attitudes and emotions requires a great deal of courage. The rewards, however, are worth the discomfort.

Honest confrontations with your shadow can help reduce splits in your mind and unlock more of your creative potential. In other words, courage opens up a new world of possibilities for personal growth. So, if you're feeling stuck, remember that it takes courage to move forward. And the rewards just might be worth it.

Cultivate Self-Compassion

According to Buddhism, it is important to cultivate a sense of friendliness towards oneself before attempting to get to know one's shadow. This concept, called Maitrī , is based on the idea that it is difficult to look at our darker aspects if we do not have a basic level of self-compassion and acceptance. If we are constantly striving for perfection or beating ourselves up for mistakes, we will never be able to confront our shadows.

Conversely, if we think too highly of ourselves, we may not be able to see our shadows accurately. In both cases, self-compassion is key. By accepting ourselves—flaws and all—we can begin to explore the parts of ourselves that we have been hiding away. At some point in our lives, we will all find ourselves amid a difficult situation. Whether it's a personal conflict, a professional setback, or simply the result of bad luck, these challenges can leave us feeling lost and alone. It's important to remember that we are not alone in these moments.

Everyone has struggles and everyone makes mistakes. As the famous saying goes, "to err is human." What's important is how we deal with these challenges. Do we face them head-on, or do we try to ignore them? If we try to ignore them, they will only become bigger and more powerful. The first step to dealing with our challenges is to accept them. Only then can we begin to work through them. Remember, you are not alone in this. We all have shadows, and we all have difficulties. But when we face them with courage and compassion, we can overcome anything.

Reclaim Your Projections Over and Over.

The act of projection is something that we are all guilty of, albeit unconsciously. It's only natural to want to protect ourselves from hurt and pain by deflecting certain emotions and qualities onto other people or objects. However, this defense mechanism can often do more harm than good.

By repressing aspects of our personality that we deem to be undesirable, we only amplify their power. These hidden parts of ourselves can fester and grow, eventually leading to feelings of resentment and anger.

It's human nature to project our own qualities onto others, especially those who trigger strong reactions in us. We may see qualities in them that we don't like or that we're not aware of in ourselves. These projections act as a barrier to truly seeing the other person, and they can lead to misunderstanding and conflict. If we can become aware of our projections, we can begin to take them back and integrate them into our consciousness. This is not an easy process, but it's essential for growth and for perceiving reality more clearly. Otherwise, we'll be stuck reacting to the world around us without really understanding it or ourselves.

Record Your Discoveries

It's interesting how some aspects of ourselves that we've disowned still want to remain out of our awareness. It's as if they're slipping out of our minds, just like a dream slips out of our minds moments after we wake up. But even after we catch them, they can still elude us. Keeping a writing journal where you record your discoveries about yourself can be a remedy for this. Just be sure to review your insights and findings later on so you can help encode them into your awareness. Doing this will allow you to better understand yourself and make more informed decisions about your life.

What to Expect

Starting Shadow Work can feel like learning a new skill. However, as you get more comfortable with the process, it starts to feel more natural. You begin to realize that you're not just learning about yourself, but you're also integrating your shadow. In other words, you're making peace with the part of yourself that you've been ignoring, repressing, or denying.

This doesn't mean that your shadow is suddenly all rainbows and butterflies. But you might find that as you become more accepting of your shadow, it becomes less shadowy. The light of your consciousness illuminates the dark corners of your psyche, and you can start to see your shadow in a new, more positive light.

In order to begin integrating your shadow, it is first important to become aware of when it is expressing itself. This may be easier said than done, as you may already know that you have certain qualities that could be considered negative, but not be aware of when they are actually manifesting. However, catching your shadow in the act is a significant step in the right direction, as it begins to reduce the split between your conscious and unconscious selves. With this awareness, you can start to regulate your shadow qualities, rather than them running rampant. In other words, you can begin to take back control. While it may be difficult to face up to your shadow side, doing so can be incredibly liberating and help you to lead a more balanced life.

Key Takeaways from Shadow Work

Benefits of Shadow Work

- Acceptance
- Authenticity
- Awakening
- Compassion
- Courage
- Creativity
- Emotional Freedom
- Empowering Yourself
- Heightened Intuition
- Improved Immune System
- Improved Relationships
- Seeing More Clearly
- Self-Understanding
- Sense Of Purpose

Methods for Shadow Work

- Try meditation to center yourself.
- Be fearless in your honesty.
- Consider your emotional reactions (triggers).
- Rediscover your childhood.
- Observe yourself objectively.
- Keep a journal as frequently as possible.
- Openly communicate with others around you.
- Discover beneficial patterns and habits.
- Accept the things you can't alter or control.

Shadow Self-Emotions

Although everyone is different and there is no set method for healing and Shadow Work, there are a few stages that might assist, which are as follows:

1. Figure out who you are and where you are.
2. Connect your emotions to how you feel.
3. Link the feelings to specific events or patterns.
4. Reflect on and comprehend these emotions.
5. Develop a new pattern or direction.

Part 2

Your Journey into Shadow Work

"Your Shadow is all of the things, 'positive' and 'negative', that you've denied about yourself and hidden beneath the surface of the mask you forgot that you're wearing."

- Oli Anderson

How to Get Started

Step 1: Choose an Aspect of Your Shadow

Judgment is human nature. We often dislike people for qualities we do not like in ourselves. If we take the time to pay attention to our reactions, we can learn a lot about ourselves. Our shadow side is the part of ourselves that we have not yet accepted. It is essential to get to know our shadow side and make peace with it. Only then can we move forward in life and relationships. The next time you judge someone, take a step back and ask yourself what it is about them that bothers you.

Whatever irritates you in another person is very likely a disowned part of yourself. Get to know that component, embrace it, and make it a part of you; the next time you see it in someone else, it may not elicit such a strong emotional response. So, in Step 1, think about someone you know (spouse, friend, cousin, boss) and pick anything that frustrates you about them. You probably already have someone in mind.) Don't choose something trivial, like the volume of their laugh or the speed of their walk; instead, find a defining personality characteristic of theirs. For example, maybe you think one of your buddies is arrogant or a slacker or passive-aggressive.

Step 2: Examine Yourself for That Attribute or Behavior

When working with your shadow, keep in mind that what is in one of us is in all of us. True, not everyone exhibits every behavioral characteristic all of the time. But every quality—the good, the bad, and the ugly—is present in all of us, waiting for the appropriate circumstances to activate it.

So, the next step is to call into mind the qualities you notice in others (from Step 1). Assume you're passing judgment on a buddy who is sluggish. He sits about all day, refuses to work, ignores his physical health, and so on. Was there ever a period in your life when you were a slacker? Perhaps things weren't going your way and you began to lose hope or give up.

We are all prone to laziness. We all have a part of us that wants to do nothing except enjoy transitory pleasures. You wouldn't mind someone else's laziness unless you're denying your own. You'll be less frustrated with your friend once you recognize the laziness within.

Step 3: Conduct an Inner Dialogue

Many types of inner work need an active discussion with various aspects of oneself.

This may appear to be a frightening concept at first since we have the misconception that only "mad people" talk to themselves. However, we all have multiple subpersonalities— numerous unacknowledged, independent aspects of our minds.

Several integrative therapies are available to help with these dissimilar aspects, including

- Jung's Active Imagination
- Schwartz's Internal Family Systems
- Stone and Winkelman's Voice Dialogue
- Assagioli's Psychosynthesis

The elements of ourselves that we are unaware of are characteristics of our shadow. They have a way of affecting our conduct when we don't pay attention to them.

Have you ever done something or said something and then questioned why you did or said it? An archetype or part of you was in command. Every "accident" is an archetype taking over your conduct.

Who hasn't engaged in self-sabotage?

Our disowned parts aren't intentionally aiming to harm us, but when we ignore or deny them, they frequently do.

We may combine these distinct sections into our conscious mind by conversing with them in our imagination or in a notebook. Then they become our allies rather than our adversaries.

So, in this step, talk to the part of yourself that you acknowledged in Step 2. Learn about that lazy bit, for example. Examine what it expects from you, what it enjoys, and how it feels about the way you spend your life.

Among the most important questions are:

- Who am I?
- What's important to me?
- What do I want from myself?
- What am I trying to show myself?

Be patient and receptive to what this part of yourself has to offer.

Step 4: Restore the Disowned Quality in You

Finally, become this characteristic or feature. In the example of laziness, imagine yourself as someone who is occasionally lazy. Remember that no single characteristic identifies you. By suppressing our shadow, we make the mistake of denying that many of these attributes exist inside us. That is why we project them onto others, become upset, and pass judgment on them. Owning a "darker" aspect of yourself, like Step 3, may seem uncomfortable since you're accepting something conflicting with your self-identity. As a result, your ego will instinctively oppose it.

You can create assertions to yourself or speak them out, such as:

- I am a slacker
- I am arrogant
- I am foolish
- I am envious
- I am dull
- I am intelligent
- I am funny

The latter two examples are good traits, as the shadow may disclose beneficial suppressed qualities that we project on others.

Experience the part of yourself that exhibits these characteristics as thoroughly as possible. Avoid making the process abstract or conceptual; instead, simply BE it. You may now reclaim and incorporate this characteristic inside yourself.

Part 3

The Workbook

"We all have a dark side. Most of us go through life avoiding direct confrontation with that aspect of ourselves, which I call the shadow self. There's a reason why. It carries a great deal of energy."

- Lorraine Toussaint

Mind Mapping

Most of us go through our days on autopilot, reacting to the
world around us instead of being proactive in managing our own
lives. Mind mapping is a great way to become more aware of
your thoughts and emotions and to start making decisions based
on what you **want** rather than what others **expect of you**.

This exercise can be done regularly as a way to get in touch with
your thoughts and feelings and to track changes over time. It can
also be helpful for problem-solving—if you're struggling with a
particular issue, mind mapping can help you brainstorm possible
solutions.

Make a list of the feelings you experience and the thoughts that
accompany them. The most essential thing here is to examine
oneself objectively. If you sense judgment appearing, take note
of that as well, but try for a more neutral vibe. Simply write a
couple of words about how you are feeling.

19.3.24 Day 1 Deeply tired, stressed, anxious

Day 2 _____

Day 3 _____

Day 4 _____

Day 5 _____

Day 6 _____

Day 7 _____

What are the most prevalent thoughts? What is the typical ratio
of lighter to heavier emotions? Is there a pattern in external
factors that cause mood fluctuations, such as a certain
individual, or events that trigger specific emotions?

19,3
24

Day 1:

Difficult thoughts are more prevelant than
lighter more optimistic thoughts. This time
last year there were No! light or positive thoughts
a year of therapy has helped. Most prevalent
thoughts are how difficult my life feels,
how much I am deeply struggling physically.
Willing myself constantly to get tasks done,
worrying about how unwell I feel and will feel
for the rest of the day, how much of a struggle
my further tasks of the day will be. anxious
about not being able to show up how I wish
I could. Almost everything is a trigger!

What do you believe are some of your most limiting beliefs
based on your observations? Which of the following are some of
your most powerful beliefs?

I do not see or feel any limiting beliefs as
they are all accurate and simply the truth.

If I am aware of my experience and my
internal dialogue is a description of
my experience, my belief is just
my understanding of my experience

Is believing in my experience limiting
me?
How could I not believe in it?

Self-Regulation From the Bottom-Up

I recommend practicing self-regulation before and throughout any Shadow Work to stay grounded and focused when dealing with painful and sensitive themes. Top-down approaches to nervous system regulation seek to quiet the mind in order to relax the body, whereas bottom-up approaches seek to relax the body first in order to calm the mind.

Using both feelings and thoughts to process past events can assist a person in realizing that the threat to which they are responding is actually old. You can begin to acquire awareness, putting the threat behind you. This approach can help you develop dual consciousness in that you can use it to keep yourself safe in the present while also reflecting on what has happened in the past. This healing process permits a sense of safety in the current day to develop a sense of safety in the younger portions of the self, which would otherwise only know danger as constant.

Simply become aware of tension in the body and relax the appropriate muscles to practice the bottom-up approach of self-regulation. Use the following checklist to travel around your body and simply notice areas of tension.

- Forehead
- Eyes
- Neck
- Shoulders
- The upper back
- The lower back
- The lower abdomen
- Thighs
- Calves

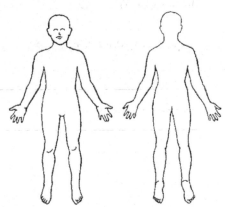

Consider how you feel about your mental clarity and emotional well-being before addressing any problems. On a scale of 1 to 10, with 1 being the best and 10 being the worst, rate yourself. Do not overthink your responses; instead, put down the first number that comes to mind.

Mental clarity: ＿＿＿

Emotional well-being:

_____

_____

_____

_____

_____

_____

_____

Take a few deep breaths and direct your attention to releasing tension in the areas noted by the checklist. Breathe and calm yourself, concentrating on melting away the tension in those muscles. After that, assess your feelings again on a scale from 1 to 10. Keep track of any ideas and feelings you have concerning the difference before and after self-regulation.

Mental Clarity: ＿＿＿

Emotional Well-Being:

_____

_____

_____

_____

_____

_____

_____

Emotional Triggers

Negative emotions, regardless of mental health, are a natural part of existence. Something can happen on any given day to disturb, frighten, or anger a person. However, occasionally people experience similar feelings for no apparent reason. In such circumstances, emotional triggers may be the cause of sudden, unfavorable mood swings.

An emotional trigger is something—a subject, a word, or even a memory—that elicits very intense unpleasant sentiments in you. Triggers frequently impact people independently of their overall state, making them more upsetting for people dealing with mental health disorders.

Triggers, for example, can generate a wide range of unpleasant feelings, including:

- Fear
- Sadness
- Anger
- Insecurity
- Anxiety

The reaction to a trigger is not purely mental. Emotional triggers can cause physical symptoms that resemble those of an anxiety condition. Physical manifestations of triggers include:

- Accelerated heart rate
- Nausea
- Shaking
- Dizziness
- Sweating palms

Use the space below to think about your triggers, feel free to list or even draw them!

Choose one trigger from the last exercise to work with, and take a minute to recall when you first became reactive to that person, location, item, topic, or scenario. What is the underlying reason for the trigger? Write about your experience after you've found the fundamental reason.

_____
_____
_____
_____
_____
_____
_____
_____
_____
_____
_____

The Past

Because the past may influence the present and shape your future, it is critical to understand it on a deep level.

What prior occurrence do I believe is still having an impact on my life today?

_____

_____

_____

_____

_____

_____

_____

_____

_____

_____

Why and how is this hurting me?

_____

_____

_____

_____

_____

_____

_____

_____

_____

_____

How can I recover by working through this?

_____

_____

_____

_____

_____

_____

_____

_____

_____

_____

_____

_____

Everyone Has an Inner Child.

This inner child might be a genuine portrayal of yourself in your childhood, a patchwork collection of developmental phases you've lived through, or a representation of young dreams and playfulness. An awareness of your inner child might assist you in remembering happier times. However, not everyone identifies childhood with playfulness and enjoyment. If you have suffered from neglect, trauma, or other forms of emotional pain, your inner child may appear little, fragile, and in need of care. You may have buried this pain deeply in order to conceal it and protect yourself.

Hiding suffering does not make it go away. Instead, it frequently manifests in your adult life as pain in personal relationships or problems satisfying your own needs. Some of these difficulties can be addressed by working to repair your inner child.

Healing your inner child might take time, but these eight suggestions are an excellent place to start.

In this book, we will go over several exercises that will not only help you understand your inner child better but will also help you to heal any wounds that this part of yourself might have.

1) Open a Channel With Your Inner Child

The first effective inner child healing technique is to close your eyes and journey back to your childhood.

Consider five things that made you joyful when you were younger. For example:

- Having fun with your siblings
- Eating amazing food
- Running through the woods
- Feeling insatiably curious
- Participating in sports

These may be really basic activities that you did as a child that made you happy. Reliving memories in your thoughts connect you to your inner child; the more innocent and emotionally vulnerable aspect of yourself that still remains.

It's okay if you use photos of your younger self to help you with the exercise! However, the emphasis here is on the feelings and situations that brought you joy.

Your inner child resides within you and is you. He or she would welcome the opportunity for adult you to reconnect and express your gratitude for the same things you formerly did.

The inner child's communication channel is now more open.

_____

_____

_____

_____

_____

_____

_____

_____

_____

_____

_____

2) Interview Your Inner Child

There are three types of inner children: the abandoned child, the anxious child, and the playful child.

1. The abandoned inner child received little affection and attention.

This might be due to their parents being too busy, abusive, or inattentive. The abandoned child is scared of being regarded as unworthy and being left out, left behind, and without affection.

2. The anxious inner child is afraid of being seen as insufficient.

They were subjected to a great deal of criticism from a young age, which left them yearning for validation and approval. Even the tiniest sense of being "bad" or "not good enough" causes them great pain.

3. The playful inner child was raised without many responsibilities.

Their childhood was defined by having fun, being free, being cared for, and feeling spontaneous and joyous. Adult life's constraints, judgments, and regulations might leave the playful inner child confused and frustrated.

* * *

It is your responsibility to seek and reach out to your inner child. Look them in the eyes and ask them how they are feeling. Then you'll know what sort of inner child you are, and we can move on to the third phase.

What words do you wish you had heard as a child? How would your life have been different if you had heard them?

_____

_____

_____

_____

_____

_____

_____

_____

_____

_____

_____

3) Take Out a Pen and Paper and Prepare to Write...

Following that is a strong writing practice that is excellent for inner child healing.

Write a letter to your inner child with a pen and paper.

This is your apology for the ways you've evaluated and undervalued your inner child, especially focusing on devaluing their appearance.

DATE: _____

Letter to my Inner Child

_____
_____
_____
_____
_____
_____
_____
_____
_____
_____
_____
_____
_____
_____
_____
_____
_____
_____
_____
_____

4) Recognize Your Inner Child's Worries and Beliefs.

Your inner child is a person who is quite similar to you, especially because *they are you*. Your inner child is not the same as the "kid" version of yourself; they are the subconscious and less-formed version of yourself who still lives up in your brain. This means that they are the true essence of who you have become.

Our inner child is not yet fully formed, but they are the real deal. They experienced the things that made us into who we are. They can help us understand our fears and pain. Our inner child doesn't filter their thoughts and feelings as we as adults do, which means they can give us honest feedback.

They live life as it happens, and ideas that we transfer into our inner child can create significant confusion and grief.

Identifying your inner child's ideas and anxieties is the first step toward connecting with them. These are frequently manifested as emotions and imprecise feelings. For example:

- "I feel vulnerable and uncomfortable."
- "I don't think I'm good enough."
- "I feel like I'm falling behind."
- "I feel ignored."
- "I have the impression that I am utterly alone."

Be honest with yourself about what your inner child is saying to you, and wrestle with it as much as you need to.

This effort will teach you a fresh perspective on how deep the roots of feeling unattractive may go. Try to put some distance between yourself and the belief.

Instead of expressing to yourself, "I feel inadequate," say, "The wounded inner child within me feels inadequate."

Consider the notion without identifying it as good or terrible, correct or incorrect. This will assist you in seeing your thoughts for what they are: thoughts.

Write them here:

_____

_____

_____

_____

_____

_____

_____

_____

_____

_____

Memories from Childhood

Childhood experiences engraved into the subconscious may influence many aspects of life without you even realizing it; meditating on your childhood recollections might assist.

Positive childhood experiences that have influenced your life:

_____

_____

_____

_____

_____

_____

_____

_____

_____

_____

What emotions are linked with these pleasant memories?

_____

_____

_____

_____

_____

_____

_____

_____

_____

_____

Negative childhood experiences that have had an impact on your life:

_____

_____

_____

_____

_____

_____

_____

_____

_____

_____

_____

What emotions are linked with these traumatic memories?

_____

_____

_____

_____

_____

_____

_____

_____

_____

_____

_____

What impact did these events have on you as a person and your life today?

_____

_____

_____

_____

_____

_____

_____

_____

_____

_____

_____

What actions can you take to reconcile yourself to these events and memories?

_____

_____

_____

_____

_____

_____

_____

_____

_____

_____

_____

Dealing with Limiting Beliefs

Limiting beliefs are erroneous ideas that keep us from achieving our dreams and ambitions. Limiting beliefs might prevent you from doing critical things like applying for your ideal job or finding (alternatively, leaving) a relationship.

Limiting beliefs are often classified into three types:

- Limiting thoughts **about yourself** that make you feel like you can't achieve something because you're flawed in some way.
- Limiting worldviews **about society** that make you feel like you can't achieve anything because no one will allow you.
- Beliefs that make you believe you can't achieve anything because it's too tough.

A limiting belief system is frequently the source of the harmful loops from which many individuals feel unable to break free. It's a running narrative that you might not be aware of, but it can have a significant influence on your day-to-day existence.

List here some limiting beliefs you might have:

_____

_____

_____

_____

_____

_____

_____

_____

_____

How to Get Rid of Your Limiting Beliefs

Identifying your limiting beliefs can be hard. Overcoming them can be even harder. But it is possible. Here are some basic steps to help you get started.

1. Consider the question, "What if I'm wrong?"
Adopt the capacity to simply challenge your own views and consider different options. Consider imagining a scenario in which your assumption is incorrect.

2. Consider the question "How is this belief serving me?"
We want to think of ourselves as victims of our own limiting beliefs, but the fact is that we embrace them to help us in some manner. The elephant feels she is unable to break away from the fence post because that notion formerly benefitted her—it saved her from the pressure and effort of failing.

In general, we hold onto limiting beliefs to shelter ourselves from difficulty and failure.

Beliefs only stick if they assist us in some manner; consider how your belief serves you and whether it is truly worth it.

3. Construct Alternative Beliefs

It's now time to be creative.

Consider all the ways you may be incorrect. Sure, the typical person might not be attracted to someone your height, but you're not looking for the average person; you're looking for someone exceptional. And someone special will find you appealing just the way you are.

Sure, you're older than most individuals starting a new job, but who says you can't be successful? Nothing except your own mentality stands in your way.

Now you're developing the habit of questioning your ideas (steps 1 and 2 above) and experimenting with new ones. It can even help to write these down. Make a list of 4-5 viable alternatives to your assumption, and then write them down.

_____

_____

_____

_____

_____

_____

_____

_____

_____

_____

_____

_____

_____

_____

_____

_____

_____

_____

This causes you to recognize that you not only have certain restricting ideas but that you also have alternatives. Even if you don't know it, you choose what you believe in every moment of your life.

4. Put those alternative beliefs to the test to see if they are true.

The final step is to consider these different ideas as hypotheses in an experiment. Now, if you can, it's up to you to put them to the test and discover whether they "work."

We can't know what is true and what isn't unless we are prepared to test these different views in the real world. And, most of the time, we discover that our initial assumptions were incorrect.

It only requires self-awareness to contemplate that we may have been mistaken and the bravery to go out into the world and discover if we were mistaken.

Dreamwork

Psychologist Carl Jung believed that the secrets of the shadow are revealed and symbolically expressed in dreams. Jung believed that by understanding the symbols in our dreams, we can gain insights into our shadow selves.

Everybody has at least one recurring dream. Give yourself some time to think, and describe one of yours (don't worry if you can't remember!). Consider what you believe the underlying significance of this dream is while you write. During this exploratory period, trust your gut and avoid second-guessing yourself.

- Who appears in your dream?
- What are you doing in your dream, and why are you doing it?
- In your dream, how do you feel?
- In your dream, where are you?
- Is there anything noteworthy in your dream, such as items, animals, or symbols?
- Is there anything more you want to mention about your dream?

Write about your recurring dream:

_____

_____

_____

_____

_____

_____

_____

_____

_____

_____

_____

_____

_____

_____

_____

_____

_____

_____

_____

_____

_____

_____

_____

_____

_____

_____

_____

_____

_____

_____

_____

Patterns

Patterns may also become habits as they are intertwined into your life; breaking patterns is more difficult than creating new ones but recognizing and working through them is critical for progress.

What patterns/habits do you find yourself repeating the most?

_____
_____
_____
_____
_____
_____
_____
_____
_____
_____
_____

How do you feel about this?

_____
_____
_____
_____
_____
_____
_____
_____
_____
_____
_____

What habits/patterns do you believe you acquired from your parents?

_____

_____

_____

_____

_____

_____

_____

_____

_____

_____

The following are some steps I can take to break these habits/patterns:

_____

_____

_____

_____

_____

_____

_____

_____

_____

_____

Things I believe I will struggle with the most are:

_____

_____

_____

_____

_____

_____

_____

_____

_____

_____

_____

_____

Healing

Healing is a complex process with many levels; taking time to dwell on various feelings and ideas can aid in the healing of internal wounds.

Do I engage in any self-destructive behavior or is there a person or event that is limiting my full potential?

_____

_____

_____

_____

_____

_____

_____

_____

_____

_____

_____

Write any negative word that appeared in the paragraph above

_____

_____

_____

_____

_____

_____

_____

_____

_____

_____

_____

What is preventing me from healing as a result of these things/people/events?

_____

_____

_____

_____

_____

_____

_____

_____

_____

_____

_____

Methods that can assist me in healing include:

_____

_____

_____

_____

_____

_____

_____

_____

_____

_____

_____

Write any positive word that appeared in the paragraph above

_____

_____

_____

_____

_____

_____

_____

_____

_____

_____

_____

I have recovered from the following things/people/events:

_____

_____

_____

_____

_____

_____

_____

_____

_____

_____

_____

_____

Reflection

Reflection is an important part of Shadow Work because it helps you to fully examine yourself and your life, determining what you desire and what no longer serves you.

Which aspects of yourself do you believe you have lost and wish to reclaim?

_____

_____

_____

_____

_____

_____

_____

_____

_____

_____

Is there anything you take for granted, and if so, what and why?

_____

_____

_____

_____

_____

_____

_____

_____

_____

_____

What are you doing about the most important things in your life?

_____

_____

_____

_____

_____

_____

_____

_____

_____

_____

_____

When was the last or most important time you pushed the boundaries of your comfort zone?

_____

_____

_____

_____

_____

_____

_____

_____

_____

_____

Radical Self-Acceptance

The more love and acceptance you can provide to all sides of your being, the better you will be able to access and implement the lessons learned from your shadow. Working through this exercise will allow you to develop radical self-acceptance.

List five things you struggle to love about yourself:

_____

_____

_____

_____

_____

_____

_____

_____

List five things you love about yourself:

_____

_____

_____

_____

_____

_____

_____

_____

Are there aspects of yourself that you find unlovable? _____

What exactly are they?

_____

_____

_____

_____

_____

_____

_____

_____

Would these behaviors, attitudes, or attributes make someone else (i.e. your mother, a friend, a stranger) unlovable in your opinion? ____

If not, why do you believe you can tolerate these traits in others but cannot accept them in yourself?

_____

_____

_____

_____

_____

_____

_____

_____

_____

_____

_____

How can you be more accepting of your flaws?

_____

_____

_____

_____

_____

_____

_____

_____

_____

_____

_____

Forgiveness

Forgiveness is essential for mental clarity and general self-care; carrying grudges or thoughts of hatred may weight on the spirit, slowly sinking you over time.

Have you forgiven those who have wronged you? Why or why not?

_____

_____

_____

_____

_____

_____

_____

_____

_____

_____

_____

Do you find it difficult to forgive others, and if so, why?

_____

_____

_____

_____

_____

_____

_____

_____

_____

_____

_____

Do you keep a grudge, and if so, for how long have you kept it?

_____

_____

_____

_____

_____

_____

_____

_____

_____

_____

_____

Is it better to harbor a grudge toward someone or yourself? Why?

_____

_____

_____

_____

_____

_____

_____

_____

_____

_____

_____

What measures can I take to work on forgiving myself?

_____

_____

_____

_____

_____

_____

_____

_____

_____

_____

_____

_____

How does forgiving others or yourself make you feel?

_____

_____

_____

_____

_____

_____

_____

_____

_____

_____

_____

Part 4

The Letters to self

Be who you are and say what you feel because those who mind
don't matter and those who matter don't mind. Don't cry
because it's over. Smile because it happened.

- Dr. Seuss

APOLOGY - LETTER TO SELF

An apology letter is a letter expressing regret or remorse for an error, offense, or other failures. The purpose of an apology letter is to recognize the mistake and help release bottled-up feelings such as guilt, self-doubt, blame, etc... Begin by acknowledging the wrong that was done, without making excuses. By taking these steps, you can begin to repair the damage you have done and move forward with a sense of purpose. Write an apology letter to yourself.

DATE: _____

_____

_____

_____

_____

_____

_____

_____

_____

_____

_____

_____

_____

_____

_____

_____

_____

_____

_____

_____

What makes you feel strong? How do you accept your true self, even if it differs from what others expect?

_____

_____

_____

_____

_____

_____

_____

_____

_____

_____

_____

_____

_____

_____

_____

_____

_____

_____

_____

_____

_____

_____

_____

_____

_____

_____

_____

_____

FORGIVENESS - LETTER TO SELF

One way to work through feelings of anger, resentment, or betrayal is to write a forgiveness letter to yourself. This can be a powerful exercise in self-compassion and understanding. When writing a letter, it is important, to be honest and direct about what happened and how it made you feel. However, it is also important to maintain a sense of perspective and refrain from self-blame. After all, we are all human and make mistakes. Once you have written the letter, you may choose to read it aloud or destroy it as a symbol of letting go. The most important thing is that you allow yourself the space to forgive.

DATE: _____

_____

_____

_____

_____

_____

_____

_____

_____

_____

_____

_____

_____

_____

_____

_____

_____

_____

_____

_____

Is there anything that can be done to reverse what has occurred? How can you take advantage of this growth opportunity?

_____

_____

_____

_____

_____

_____

_____

_____

_____

_____

_____

_____

_____

_____

_____

_____

_____

_____

_____

_____

_____

_____

_____

_____

_____

_____

_____

_____

_____

_____

SELF LOVE - LETTER TO SELF

Before you begin writing your love letter, take some time to reflect on what you love about yourself. What are your best qualities? What have you accomplished that you are proud of? Write down a list of things you love about yourself, inside and out. Once you have your list, it's time to start writing. Begin by addressing yourself by name, and then express your love for yourself.

Use positive affirmations and reassuring phrases to build yourself up. In your letter, affirm that you accept and appreciate yourself just the way you are. Remind yourself that you are perfect just as you are, and that you deserve all the love in the world. Let yourself know that it is okay to make mistakes - we all do - and that you will always be deserving of love, no matter what happens.

Finish your letter by expressing gratitude for having the chance to love yourself. Thank yourself for being strong, for being alive, and for being YOU.

Writing a love letter to yourself can be a powerful act of self-care and self-love. By expressing your adoration for who you are, you are affirming your worthiness and showing yourself some much-needed compassion. So go ahead - give it a try! You might just be surprised at how good it feels.

DATE: _____

What brings you joy?

_____

_____

_____

_____

_____

_____

_____

_____

_____

_____

_____

_____

_____

_____

_____

_____

_____

_____

_____

_____

_____

_____

_____

_____

_____

_____

_____

_____

_____

Part 5 The Shadow Prompts

Growth is painful. Change is painful. But, nothing is as painful as staying stuck where you do not belong.

N. R. Narayana Murthy

How do I define happiness?

What valuable lessons have I learned so far?

How do I feel about my relationship with my mother?

_____
_____
_____
_____
_____
_____
_____
_____
_____
_____
_____
_____
_____
_____
_____
_____
_____
_____
_____
_____
_____
_____
_____
_____
_____
_____
_____

When have I been a hypocrite?

Am I allowing others to use me as an emotional punching bag?

_____

_____

_____

_____

_____

_____

_____

_____

_____

_____

_____

_____

_____

_____

_____

_____

_____

_____

_____

_____

_____

_____

_____

_____

_____

_____

_____

What subjects, in particular, do I avoid? Why?

Describe a time when rejection resulted in re-direction.

What aspects of my future do I find most exciting?

_____

_____

_____

_____

_____

_____

_____

_____

_____

_____

_____

_____

_____

_____

_____

_____

_____

_____

_____

_____

_____

_____

_____

_____

_____

_____

What is my favorite thing in my life?

If applicable, what did my most recent romantic relationship teach me?

_____
_____
_____
_____
_____
_____
_____
_____
_____
_____
_____
_____
_____
_____
_____
_____
_____
_____
_____
_____
_____
_____
_____
_____
_____
_____
_____
_____
_____

How do I feel about my relationship with my father?

_____
_____
_____
_____
_____
_____
_____
_____
_____
_____
_____
_____
_____
_____
_____
_____
_____
_____
_____
_____
_____
_____
_____
_____
_____

When was the last time I made a negative comment about someone behind their back?

_____
_____
_____
_____
_____
_____
_____
_____
_____
_____
_____
_____
_____
_____
_____
_____
_____
_____
_____
_____
_____
_____
_____
_____
_____

When was the last time I got criticized? How did I feel?

_____

_____

_____

_____

_____

_____

_____

_____

_____

_____

_____

_____

_____

_____

_____

_____

_____

_____

_____

_____

_____

_____

_____

_____

_____

_____

When was the last time I did something damaging to myself?

For what am I grateful?

_____

_____

_____

_____

_____

_____

_____

_____

_____

_____

_____

_____

_____

_____

_____

_____

_____

_____

_____

_____

_____

_____

_____

_____

_____

_____

_____

_____

_____

What qualities do I admire the most in others?

_____

_____

_____

_____

_____

_____

_____

_____

_____

_____

_____

_____

_____

_____

_____

_____

_____

_____

_____

_____

_____

_____

_____

_____

_____

_____

_____

What was the most heartbreaking event in my life?

_____

_____

_____

_____

_____

_____

_____

_____

_____

_____

_____

_____

_____

_____

_____

_____

_____

_____

_____

_____

_____

_____

_____

_____

_____

_____

_____

What are my current short-term objectives?

How can I express gratitude for the changes in my life?

When am I the most critical of myself?

_____

_____

_____

_____

_____

_____

_____

_____

_____

_____

_____

_____

_____

_____

_____

_____

_____

_____

_____

_____

_____

_____

_____

_____

_____

_____

_____

_____

What am I addicted to?

_____

_____

_____

_____

_____

_____

_____

_____

_____

_____

_____

_____

_____

_____

_____

_____

_____

_____

_____

_____

_____

_____

_____

_____

What are my current long-term objectives?

What part of myself do I keep hidden from others?

_____

_____

_____

_____

_____

_____

_____

_____

_____

_____

_____

_____

_____

_____

_____

_____

_____

_____

_____

_____

_____

_____

_____

_____

_____

What area of my personality do I feel still needs to be improved?

What does confidence mean to me?

What is keeping me from doing something I've wanted to accomplish for a long time?

_____

_____

_____

_____

_____

_____

_____

_____

_____

_____

_____

_____

_____

_____

_____

_____

_____

_____

_____

_____

_____

_____

_____

On which occasions have I said yes when I should have said no?

_____

_____

_____

_____

_____

_____

_____

_____

_____

_____

_____

_____

_____

_____

_____

_____

_____

_____

_____

_____

_____

_____

_____

_____

What do I need to forgive myself for?

In what areas have I improved in over the past year?

_____
_____
_____
_____
_____
_____
_____
_____
_____
_____
_____
_____
_____
_____
_____
_____
_____
_____
_____
_____
_____
_____
_____
_____
_____

What helps me relax when I'm upset?

_____

_____

_____

_____

_____

_____

_____

_____

_____

_____

_____

_____

_____

_____

_____

_____

_____

_____

_____

_____

_____

_____

_____

_____

_____

_____

_____

Who is a member of my inner circle? Do they make me happy?

_____

_____

_____

_____

_____

_____

_____

_____

_____

_____

_____

_____

_____

_____

_____

_____

_____

_____

_____

_____

_____

_____

_____

_____

Am I where I expected to be at this stage of my life?

Do I have any brothers or sisters? How has my connection with them evolved over the past five years?

_____
_____
_____
_____
_____
_____
_____
_____
_____
_____
_____
_____
_____
_____
_____
_____
_____
_____
_____
_____
_____
_____
_____
_____
_____

What changes have occurred in my relationship with my parents during the past five years?

_____

_____

_____

_____

_____

_____

_____

_____

_____

_____

_____

_____

_____

_____

_____

_____

_____

_____

_____

_____

_____

_____

_____

_____

Can I recall somebody I detested ten years ago? Does it matter now?

Write your parents a letter.

_____

_____

_____

_____

_____

_____

_____

_____

_____

_____

_____

_____

_____

_____

_____

_____

_____

_____

_____

_____

_____

_____

_____

_____

_____

_____

_____

_____

_____

_____

Think of a moment when I was disappointed by someone.

Think of a moment when I was deceived or abandoned.

_____
_____
_____
_____
_____
_____
_____
_____
_____
_____
_____
_____
_____
_____
_____
_____
_____
_____
_____
_____
_____
_____
_____
_____
_____
_____
_____
_____
_____
_____

When was the last time I felt totally vulnerable?

What is my worst fear? What was the source of it?

_____

_____

_____

_____

_____

_____

_____

_____

_____

_____

_____

_____

_____

_____

_____

_____

_____

_____

_____

_____

_____

_____

_____

_____

_____

_____

_____

_____

As a child, did I feel emotionally supported by my parents? Why or why not?

_____
_____
_____
_____
_____
_____
_____
_____
_____
_____
_____
_____
_____
_____
_____
_____
_____
_____
_____
_____
_____
_____
_____
_____

In life, what do I expect people to do for me?

Can I rely on others for assistance? What is my reasoning?

What do I think of my high school or college years?

_____

_____

_____

_____

_____

_____

_____

_____

_____

_____

_____

_____

_____

_____

_____

_____

_____

_____

_____

_____

_____

_____

_____

_____

_____

What lies do I tell myself?

What would I do differently if I could do it all over again?

_____
_____
_____
_____
_____
_____
_____
_____
_____
_____
_____
_____
_____
_____
_____
_____
_____
_____
_____
_____
_____
_____
_____
_____
_____
_____
_____

What is my happiest memory?

In what ways have I or others made me feel insignificant?

Can money make me happy?

What causes my anxiety?

What am I in desperate need of right now?

_____

_____

_____

_____

_____

_____

_____

_____

_____

_____

_____

_____

_____

_____

_____

_____

_____

_____

_____

_____

_____

_____

_____

_____

What would I do if there was no danger of failure?

_____
_____
_____
_____
_____
_____
_____
_____
_____
_____
_____
_____
_____
_____
_____
_____
_____
_____
_____
_____
_____
_____
_____
_____
_____
_____
_____
_____
_____

What keeps me up at night?

_____
_____
_____
_____
_____
_____
_____
_____
_____
_____
_____
_____
_____
_____
_____
_____
_____
_____
_____
_____
_____
_____
_____
_____
_____
_____
_____
_____

Am I pursuing my true passion?

How would I be seen by my 16-year-old self today?

_____

_____

_____

_____

_____

_____

_____

_____

_____

_____

_____

_____

_____

_____

_____

_____

_____

_____

_____

_____

_____

_____

_____

_____

_____

_____

_____

_____

What gets in the way of my happiness?

How do I feel about my body?

With whom would I like to talk more?

What would my ideal existence look like?

What about being an adult do I like?

_____

_____

_____

_____

_____

_____

_____

_____

_____

_____

_____

_____

_____

_____

_____

_____

_____

_____

_____

_____

_____

_____

_____

_____

_____

_____

_____

_____

_____

What causes me to be nostalgic?

Is it true that time heals all wounds?

Do I have control over my emotions, or do they have control over me?

_____

_____

_____

_____

_____

_____

_____

_____

_____

_____

_____

_____

_____

_____

_____

_____

_____

_____

_____

_____

_____

_____

_____

_____

_____

_____

_____

_____

Do I take care of myself physically and mentally?

What is the biggest "what if" that comes to my mind?

How can I tell the difference between wants and needs?

Do I have a strong connection to my culture? Why or why not?

What was the most humiliating experience of my life? Why?

_____
_____
_____
_____
_____
_____
_____
_____
_____
_____
_____
_____
_____
_____
_____
_____
_____
_____
_____
_____
_____
_____
_____
_____
_____

What is my greatest concern about my family?

_____
_____
_____
_____
_____
_____
_____
_____
_____
_____
_____
_____
_____
_____
_____
_____
_____
_____
_____
_____
_____
_____
_____
_____
_____

Do I have difficulty enforcing my boundaries? Why or why not?

_____

_____

_____

_____

_____

_____

_____

_____

_____

_____

_____

_____

_____

_____

_____

_____

_____

_____

_____

_____

_____

_____

_____

_____

_____

_____

How can I be kind to myself?

Write a letter to your ex.

_____

_____

_____

_____

_____

_____

_____

_____

_____

_____

_____

_____

_____

_____

_____

_____

_____

_____

_____

_____

_____

_____

_____

_____

_____

What was the best thing that happened to me as a child? Is it still influencing me today?

_____

_____

_____

_____

_____

_____

_____

_____

_____

_____

_____

_____

_____

_____

_____

_____

_____

_____

_____

_____

_____

_____

_____

_____

In what ways am I privileged?

Now what?

_____

_____

_____

_____

_____

_____

_____

_____

_____

_____

_____

_____

_____

_____

_____

_____

_____

_____

_____

_____

_____

_____

_____

_____

_____

_____

_____

_____

_____

A Message from the Author

First of all, thank you for reading this book. I know you could have picked any number of books to read, but you picked this book and for that, I am extremely grateful.

I hope that it's added value and quality to your life.

If you enjoyed this workbook and found benefit in going through the exercises and prompts, I'd love to hear from you and I also hope that you could take some time to post a review on the site where you purchased it from.

Your feedback and support will help me to greatly improve my writing craft for future projects and make this book even better.

Thank you,

Michelle Chira

Conclusion

Shadow Work can be difficult and requires a huge amount of emotional effort, but it's also incredibly rewarding. By facing your shadows, I hope you've learned to accept all parts of yourself and become a more whole and complete person.

I'm so glad you made it to the end of this book!

Every time someone chooses to heal themselves and grow, they contribute to collective healing. You have done a great job of healing yourself. I encourage you to continue this work and build on what you have learned.

This will make a difference in the world.

Printed in Great Britain
by Amazon

36061551R00096